My Boy Blink

My Boy Blink

Nev White

To order additional copies of this book, contact:
Xlibris Corporation
0-800-644-6988
www.xlibrispublishing.co.uk
Orders@xlibrispublishing.co.uk
305210

Contents

Dedication

To my grandchildren

PREFACE

THE STORY TAKES one from finding a baby boy amongst bracken on an early October morning in a woodland of chestnut trees to fostering years and growing up in a life of tears in the absence of love and understanding.

It is a story about his journey through life of pain suffering and uncertainty until he finds a companion in Margaret, when he joins a rambling group.

The story is peppered with incidences from the life of a boy who is tormented; it is about his will to make good and overcome disadvantages without a mum and dad and the heartache caused by a society by applying wrong decisions enforced by the State and Acts of Parliament, creating an atmosphere of turmoil, misunderstanding, dominance, and anger.

It speaks of the love and care found in other people willing to respond to a child's call for help, the acclaim from a boy who wishes to achieve something in life by playing cricket for his country.

A most enjoyable novel that could be true and worthy of a place amongst anyone's library, leaving questions: Can more be done? Who is to blame when things go wrong? The accolade, when deserved, is as true today as it will be tomorrow.

Any resemblance to anyone living or dead is purely a coincidence. It has been written with only good intentions, not to offend anyone, and all material used in this book should be accepted as what it is – a fictional story – and not meant to embarrass or insult anyone of any religion, colour, race, or physical make-up. If anyone is offended, I apologise for this is not my intention.

CHAPTER 1

A Child Is Born

'DAD, ARE THE chestnuts ready yet?'

'Yes. The time is right, usually first week in October. We'll go. Be ready for nine-thirty tomorrow. I'll put up a flask of coffee. Don't forget to bring some gloves with you this time. You know how some are prickly when in their shells. If you're quiet, we may see squirrels again.'

'Remember them foxes, Dad? I'll have camera and take photos this time. Then people will believe me.'

We arrived at the chestnut woodlands on a misty morning with split rays of autumn sunshine dazzling and dancing with colourful effects in a rolling mist disappearing into the treetops, giving a pleasing and satisfying feeling – an odd shout for a dog, an echo of children calling for their friends, pigeons cooing high in the treetops, and an odd squirrel dashing up on the blind side of a nearby tree.

'Ray, mind you, don't wonder too far, and kick those leaves about. You'll find many chestnuts fallen during the night.'

'Dad, I'm getting a lot. No one's been here. We've just come at the right time and beaten many to the fallen ones, although the car park is getting full.'

'Ray we'll have a drink soon and a biscuit or two and look at them people. Everyone seems to have same ideas as us. We must be the first.'

'No, Dad, there was that dark green car there when we arrived, and people are in it, maybe not bothered about nuts, just wanted a run out. Dad, I can hear a baby crying over there in that bracken. Come quick, Dad, over there!'

'Blinking heck, Ray! It's a baby! Give me your mobile. Better get the police and ambulance here. Get me a blanket, Ray, quick, blinking heck.'

The police arrived with a WPC. By that time, Dad had retrieved the baby from the bracken and cradled it in his arms. The WPC examined the baby and said that it was only a few hours old. Dad gave a statement, and upon this he was asked if he had seen anyone. 'No,' he answered. 'No one here when we arrived.' Dad meant we hadn't seen anyone in the woodlands.

'Dad, that car was here when we arrived, and there is someone in it.'

A policeman went over to the car to investigate; he rattled on the car door. No response. Then he quickly smashed the door window in with his baton and then shouted for assistance, but it was too late. Another police car arrived, and an ambulance took them away, blanketed over on stretchers. I was inquisitive, but Dad was trying to avoid me.

'Ray, you keep out of way.'

'What is it, Dad?'

'Just stay over there, out of the way.'

Later Dad told me that they had gassed themselves.

'What about the baby, Dad?'

'I don't know. I'm going to the police station later. Maybe they can tell me.'

Dad knew something; he wasn't telling me. He only said that in a blink of an eye the baby could have died. According to the pathologist, the woman in the car was the mother of the child and the man with her was her husband and the father of the baby. We were just in time to save its life. Dad knew much more. I wished not to ask for fear of a rebuff. I found out more by reading press releases.

Later when the baby was being considered for adoption and love it so deserved, it was given to a couple who lived about three miles away. I was puzzled that it was the same baby, and I confronted Dad. He was stubborn and grumpy. 'I know babies when I see them', he said 'and am pleased for Blink, as you call him. They are good people. I know of them. They are Mr and Mrs Sid and Joy Bloom.'

'Dad, it's not their baby. We found it. Why can't we have him? Let them have their own.'

'Ray, you'll learn when you get older. No more questions about it I understand Dad. You should be thinking about leaving school after next term and plan in what you're going to do?'

'Dad, I'm good at finding babies.'

'That's not a job!'

'It is, Dad!'

'How is it?'

'Well, they have a "missing persons" office in America. They call it Missing Persons Bureau, and here we have organisations that do similar stuff. People go missing all the time. Come to think of it, Dad, it might not be a bad idea.'

'Ray, you called the baby "Blink". Why? You have a habit of saying "blinking heck". Is it so you do not swear in front of me? When the baby was found, your first word was "blinking". So I called it Blink.'

'Dad how do you know if it's same baby that Mr and Mrs Bloom have? Ray, I do know, but I'm not telling you how. Some day maybe, but not yet, they are calling the baby Henry. I'm pleased he has a good home. He'll be well cared for and hopefully have a good life.'

'That's nice of you, Dad. I think you could have taken to Henry, and if you could, you would have loved to have him yourself.'

'That's true, Ray.'

'Dad, did you know Henry's true parents?'

'Yes, I knew them. To take their own life is difficult to understand and there may be many reasons. We should not judge others and not talk ill of others. It's so easy to criticise for many who don't understand. These kinds of people should be avoided, and they should be ashamed of their selves. Their points of view should to be ignored and deleted from their train of thoughts. I have been approached to be Henry's godfather and feel rather proud of it. I'll play my part.'

'Dad, do Mr and Mrs Bloom know what you know?'

'I don't think so, you say nothing.'

'Yes, Dad, I promise.'

CHAPTER 2

School Days, a Few Years Later

I'VE THE OPPORTUNITY to stay on at school and perhaps go for further education at college. What do you think Dad?

'Splendid! You do that. I'm all for it. What subjects would you take Ray?'

'I am interested in physical education and would love to be involved in sport learning about the body and dietary, like a fitness analyst for sport.'

So with Dad's support I studied and worked hard, and after two years obtained my scholarship for a two-year course at Oxford Universities. I felt rather proud. Then was reminded it's Henry's birthday or Blink's, as I would say, and like all other birthdays dad and wouldn't leave him out but puzzled what to buy him, we thought 'Henry is nearly old enough to start school? Shall we buy a train set, a castle, a toy garage, or do we give money? That's it! We'll give money.'

Birthdays came and another year on, Blink was ready to start school; above anything, dad and I was going to see Blink go to school on the first day of his long educational road. We felt pleased standing on the other side of the road, being unnoticed by Mums and Dads and hearing shouts of 'bye, Mum, love you' and thought how good life could be to see this once-a-baby, now growing into a pleasant child with the love and affection of carers. Soon, all children were assembled into the school. Dad paused for a moment then we turned away to go home. Dad reaching into his jacket pocket discovered a packet of mixed nuts. He took a few out and reminded me of the day of that October morning amongst the chestnut trees.

The school terms came and went; I got my diploma and now pursuing a degree that kept me away from home but dad kept me well informed on Blink saying `Blink' goes to junior school soon, and I always go at the beginning of the term and watch him go into school. 'I'm his godfather, but no one knows what I know, not even Mr and Mrs Bloom.' I often questioned myself whether to speak out; then I'd decline. It troubles me sometimes. Maybe best to leave well alone.

It was the school summer holidays, and as his godfather I was asked if I would like a trip to seaside with Mr and Mrs Bloom and Henry. I was overjoyed for Blink. We were getting very close; he got to calling me 'godfather' but his carers, whom he called Mum and Dad, cared not to hear that. It just sounded strange to hear, although it was a fact. Henry always smilingly enquired, 'Why, what's wrong with that? What do I call him, Mr Black like everyone else?'

Mrs Bloom was a gentle type of a person, always pleasant to talk to and so polite and easy to get on with; Blink couldn't have better carers as he was not adopted and the time was not right to tell him, but it may be considered when time is right.

On Sunday, we went on a trip to the seaside – a donkey ride, doughnuts, ice cream, fish and chips, and laughter all the way. 'Mr Black, this is first time I've been to the seaside. Mum and Dad are really enjoying it. Dad has brought Mum a gift. It's a musical box. It plays anniversary waltz, and I have brought you a key ring with your name on. Mr Black, how do you know of Mum and Dad?'

'Henry, I'm your dad's godfather as well as being yours. Your dad's dad was a great friend of mine. We worked together for many years in the car industry before they closed it down. Many were put out of work, but Mr. Bloom's dad and I were ready for retirement and with our redundancy money, we opened a small garage. But it's not small now.'

'No, Mr Black, that's the one that Mum and Dad share with you, a right?'

'Yes, you're right.'

'And that's your daughter Jenny who does the bookkeeping.'

'How do you know of that?'

'She told me.'

'Did she mention anything else?'

'No, Mr Black, but I'm working on it.'

The sun shone for many a bright hour. Henry wanted a swim. Mr and Mrs Bloom were ready but not me; I was far too comfortable in my deck chair. How they splashed about in the water and enjoyed teasing each other with cascades of hand-propelled water, giving off screams of happiness and joy. Upon drying off, Mr Bloom asked Henry to raise his arms. I wondered what that was.

'It's a birthmark in your armpit, not seen that before, have you, Jimmy?'

'Well, err, oh, it is nothing!'

'Yes, I know, but have you seen it before?'

'May have it's nothing to be concerned about.' And the matter was dropped, but I was reluctant to discuss the matter for only I knew the answer and that was to remain with me until I decided differently.

Time came to go home; everyone was feeling happy and contented. Henry sat in back seat of the car with me. I loved to tell jokes and little stories and then break out singing in a kind of a cantata, and now the hours of the day were catching up on us. Then all would go quiet as if reflecting upon the day of enjoyment.

It's always the same on day trips. Everyone decides to go home at the same time, causing a build-up of traffic that encourages dissent of one using up petrol, but getting nowhere. At last it was cleared, and we could move up a few gears. That was better. Thirty, forty, fifty, sixty, and then we hit the motorway; soon we'd be home – three lanes of traffic all the way home. 'No! Look out! What is it?' Brakes hard on, a quick spin and skid, a sudden bang then a long deathly silence.

Henry was protected as I threw my body over him. We were wounded and went to hospital with the rest; later, the full horrific news came through of five dead – Henry's Mum and Dad, two from another car, and one from the third car. I was allowed home but Henry was to stay in the hospital; it was the sad news that was more painful than the injuries sustained by him. He cried and cried until he could cry no more.

Social Services had to intervene, and a new home had to be found for him. In the meantime, he was to stay in a home for such people. 'Why can't I stay with Mr Black?' he would scream. But it was no use; the authorities wouldn't allow it for he was their responsibility and they would choose what was best for a seven-year-old. Whilst he was in the care home, I visited him on several occasions and was confronted with many questions: 'Why can't I live with you, grandad?'

'I'm not your grandad, my boy.'

'Well, tell them you are!'

'I can't do that.'

'Well, tell them I come and live with you.'

'No, Henry. They'll not allow it.'

'Well, what will happen to me?'

'They'll find you someone to live with. Maybe other carers for you have no family to turn to.'

'I have you, grandad.'

'You will always have me, but I'm not your grandad.'

'Well, I'm going to keep calling you my grandad. You call me your boy. What if I'm taken away? I may not see you again.'

'Henry, you know where I live, so keep in touch. Promise me that.'

'Grandad, I don't want to be adopted.'

'Henry, I have no say but I'll talk to your social worker.'

That was last time I saw of Henry.

Jenny took over running of the garage with my help in doing cosmetic work around the garage. Jenny would enquire about Henry only to hear that last they heard was they had moved away. Ray got his degree and a post at a hospital dealing with people who have various eating disorders and weight problems. No one was willing to tell him anything even if they knew anything. The last thing he did hear was that Henry had moved away to another area with guardians or adopted parents or carers; no one seemed to care or be bothered.

CHAPTER 3

Unsupported and Neglected

THREE YEARS HAD passed since Henry went away with his new guardians. Jenny, my daughter, had taken over running of the garage. I would help her in the garage by running the sales of confectionary and provisions and a doing little gardening or anything else to help out. It was here that I met Joe, a sergeant in the police force. Jenny was going out with him, and it was getting serious. I got to thinking, 'It's about time she married and settled down instead of relying on me.'

Joe asked me about Henry. 'How you know of Henry?' I asked.

'I was a constable then and was the first on the scene at the incident with the WPC. Do you not remember me? In the woods, you were gathering chestnuts.'

'Joe, he was either adopted or assigned to some guardians. It must be over three years now.'

'Would you like me to make enquiries, Mr Black?'

'Joe, if you do and find out, it might hurt his feelings. I don't know where he lives, and if I do, it may not be fair to him and may upset the social structure he finds himself in. But I would love to know.'

'Jimmy, leave it to me. I'll be discreet in my enquiries.'

'Joe, Jenny says you are going to be engaged, so when's the day?'

'We were thinking sometime next year. I require your permission. May I take this opportunity in asking you if I may marry your daughter?'

'Joe, you may! Congratulations, and thank you for asking.'

'Then we marry next spring.'

At that moment, Jenny, who was standing behind the door, listening, rushed forward and threw her arms around me in joy and thanks. A nice, pleasant atmosphere was created. I pointed to a cupboard that contained a bottle of sherry and took out three glasses. 'Jenny, please let's drink to it.'

Several months passed, and Joe mentioned that Henry had run away from his guardians and no one knew his whereabouts.

'How long has he been missing?'

'It's about a week, and Social Services think he may come to you.'

'Why should he run away?'

'We don't know.'

'From whom he's run away?'

'I don't know, Mr Black. It's Social Services that have contacted us and think maybe Henry will come to you.'

'Joe, why should he run away?'

'He lives some two hours away that I overheard, so we have to wait and see what happens. I'll keep you informed and hope you will inform me if something turns up.'

Evening came and there was a knock at the door, then a whisper, 'Grandad, it's me Henry.' on entering the house, he collapsed into my arms, full of tears. I quickly shut and locked the door behind him.

'Grandad, I have run away. Please help me!'

'Henry, what is it?'

'Grandad, it is horrible. I want to live with you.'

Henry was fatigued from absence of food and shelter. I gave him a meal and a quick shower and changed his clothes. Then I carried him to bed, were he slept soundly till nine in the morning. He devoured his breakfast of eggs, bacon, and beans with toast very quickly, eating with great mouthfuls of food, giving the impression it had been a long period since he had had a decent meal. He looked a comical young man in my shirt, which engulfed him, and slippers that were far too large. I couldn't stop laughing.

'Grandad, what`s so funny?'

'I'm not your Grandad.'

'I'm going to call you grandad. You keep calling me "my boy".'

'Henry, you remind me of Rip Van Winkle in the nursery rhymes. You only require a candle in your hand.'

Henry laughed and laughed and then cried with red watery eyes; he used the long-sleeved shirt to dry his tears, he then mumbled, 'I love you, grandad.'

'Henry, I wish to know why you ran away?'

'They beat me, refused me food, and sometimes I slept in the garden shed. They were cruel to me. I'm not going back there.'

'Henry, you have to tell me all. Henry, I'll get a pen and note things down.'

'Grandad, I got a beating every day. I was falling asleep at school and rebelled with everyone. I was unhappy, unclothed, and unfed. My beatings became constant. Look at my back. You did not see that last night, and look at these marks. They are from a stick. Look at my buttocks. Those marks are from a heavy slipper. I ran away about a week ago, and how relieved I am from the beatings. If my bruising looks bad now, imagine how they looked a week ago!'

'Wait, Henry. I've some cream. Come, I'll put some on. It'll ease your discomfort. Henry, I require names and address, and stop calling me "grandad".'

'Right grandad.'

'Henry, names please!'

Their names are 'Mr Sam Nettles and Mrs Grace Nettles. They live at Birmingham, the area and street, the address is in my trousers pocket, here.'

'Good, Henry, thank you. Now tell me, was there anyone else in the family?'

'I don't know, Grandad. People came and went. I was always pushed out of the way, sometimes in garden shed or in the garage. I was frightened to make a noise in case I received a beating. I'm not going back, Grandad. I will kill myself first.'

'Henry, we'll have less of that talk. You are not going back. You lived in Birmingham. Tell me how you got here.'

'I got a lift on the back of a lorry to near Nottingham. I stole some bread and fruit from a market stall then jumped on another lorry to Newark. At Newark, I stole some Coca-Cola and nearly got caught. I ran into the woods and stayed there for two days.'

'I was lost and hungry and met some gypsies, who fed me and comforted me. They treated me well, and Nick guided me on my way and instructed me to reach you and tell you of everything. I think he has a lot to say in the camp for many look up to him. He found me fast asleep, woke me, and took me into their camp and made me welcome.'

'Henry, why didn't he send for the police?'

'He feared the police wouldn't believe him. According to Nick, the public don't always take kindly to them because of their way of life. Nick saved my life. His mum wished me a good future and a happy life. I made my exit, unbeknown to them, not wishing to cause them trouble. Grandad, I'm here thanks to them. They wrapped some bread and cheese in a large piece of cloth, and I was on my way. They must have known what I was thinking.'

'Henry, I'm going to phone around.'

'Grandad, I'm not going back to that hellhole.'

'Cut that talk out. I have told you before, I won't let them take you. I'll ring my daughter Jenny, and a police friend of mine. Don't worry. I'll take care of you. I must inform some people of what you have told me, and how old are you?'

'Grandad, I'm ten and a half.'

'Blinking heck, you are not!'

'I am.'

I paused for a moment, then exclaimed, 'So you are! How time flies. Henry, tell me about Mr Nettles.'

'He gambles a lot. When he wins, he drinks more. When he loses, he blames me and beats me.'

'What about Mrs Nettles?'

'She's always drunk. She once told me she was a type 1 diabetic, because I saw her using a needle. But that's not true for she goes into different moods and has a lot of sugar, a spoonful and a half in her tea, and eats a lot of sweet cakes. I haven't seen any medication. I think it is dope.'

'How do you know of that?'

'Lots of boys at school talk about it, and sometimes teachers mention it. Sometimes she has parties, and I'm locked in a shed until the men go.'

'Men, you say?'

'Yes. She says they come to mend the TV or the washer has broken down. Once she said the dishwasher had broken down, but they haven't a dishwasher.'

'What do you think they were calling for, Henry?'

'Grandad, I don't know. It's awful. Don't send me back!' Henry cried and cried, and then there was a knock at the door and Henry shook in fear. But it was Jenny, whom he ran to and flung his arms around her; he just wanted some love and a cuddle.

CHAPTER 4

In Absence of Love

'JENNY, I'VE SENT for Joe. What I have to say will make your blood boil, but until Joe arrives, we'll have a cup of tea. Have you had breakfast, Jenny?'

'Yes, I'm fine with a cup of tea. What's it all about, Dad?'

'Answer the door. This could be Joe. Hello, Joe! Do you know of this young man? His name is Henry, and he's run away from his guardians at Ashby. He doesn't wish to go back. He has supplied me with information, which I have written down. Henry, this is Sergeant Roberts. He wishes to talk to you, and you have to tell him what you told me. Don't be frightened. He wishes to help you. Joe, take your coat off and have a cup of tea. Henry will have more confidence in you if you remove your coat and will feel less intimated.'

'Good idea, Jim.'

After about an hour, the sergeant whispered to me that this sad, poor lad has been through hell. 'You keep him here. I'll go and have a word with my boss, and Social Services will have to be informed. I'm undecided what to do next for the best. Don't worry, Henry. You're not in trouble. Right, I wish to make a few phone calls.'

A little later, Sergeant Joe announced he had to go to the police station to see the superintendent. 'He wishes to see you, Jimmy. We'll leave Henry with Jenny. He'll be all right.' And after a few words with Henry, we set off. Joe called at the garage and had a word with Ethel and Benny to tell them I'll be a little late. I could have given them a ring, but you can explain it better in person.

At the station, the matter was put to the superintendent. 'Jimmy, is this same lad you called "Blink"?'

'It is, but how do you know I call him Blink?'

'Jimmy, I have known you some years, and you have known me since I was a constable. Jimmy, I wish to hear the full story from you. We will then talk to Henry.'

After a lengthy discussion and statements taken and written down, the superintendent made several calls in another room and then appeared joyful. 'The boy stays with you for tonight at least. Then tomorrow we go to Ashby and have a word with Mr and Mrs Nettles. After that, we talk to the Social Services at Ashby. You come along, Jim. Will your Jenny take care of Henry whilst we go tomorrow?'

'Yes. He'll be fine.'

'What I have said about tomorrow is correct, but we'll go now to Ashby police station. Now they are aware of us, and Inspector Huw Jones will meet us. It's his patch, and he's a good man. Knowing him, he'll probably have a dossier on them. Your Jenny will be visited by Social Services just to see Henry, and if he is happy, he stays, but they may wish to see his accommodation and other things. You understand, Jim?'

'Yes, that's fine.'

'And, Jim, a doctor will be calling to see Blink and a photographer. We want photos taken of his injuries.'

'I have done that, Superintendent. Look here, I have them.'

'Good Lord! No wonder he ran, and that was nearly two weeks ago.'

On arrival at Ashby, our first job was to contact Social Services and hear what they had to say. Social Services claimed that on many occasions when they visited, nothing was out of place. When they got access, the house was clean and tidy and Henry was well presented. 'We tried a surprise visit. They didn't answer the door. We checked with the school and the head informs us that she thinks all is not well at home. This was a few weeks ago, and we haven't made contact since. Sometimes they leave messages with neighbours, saying they're going away. Now we have learnt that's not true. Why didn't you bring Henry? He could tell us more.'

'He'll be coming tomorrow. Right now, we make a few observations. We have a camcorder and wish to do a little spying. Sergeant Roberts is going to carry it out. What I wish for you to do is park your car at rear of that street. We'll be over there in ours. Sergeant Roberts is going to try to enter the property.'

Sergeant Roberts knocked at the door without getting any response. Then he forced a window open. After access, he found the occupants in bed. Then he opened front door that was heavily secured and let in the rest of the police and the social service staff. It was then they realised that the couple in bed were suffering from a drug overdose with many injection needles by their side and tablets and other paraphernalia on bedside cabinets. A doctor was sent for, but it was too late.

A Mrs Oates, a neighbour, gave much information that confirmed what Henry had said and asked about Henry. 'Poor little mite!' she said. 'What a lovely boy but always scruffy and unfed. I reported it to Social Services, but they said every time they got access, everything appeared fine.'

Social Services could only get access upon Sam and Grace's terms; when they did get access, they had paid someone to come and clean things up. You know the private companies who provide such services. Mrs Oates continued, 'I enquired about little Henry. They told me to mind my own business and that he had gone away for a few days. Many times we heard screams and cries, and from our bedroom window, we could see into their garden and see Henry being put into the garden shed. Again when we approached them, they said, "We are play-acting." We don't know if our reports to police and Social Services ever came to anything for we heard no more.'

Many people called a to the house some dressed well and some not 'we thought those with nice cars were authority like Social Services. Sam Nettles once told me they have a boarding house on the coast and many call to make bookings.'

'That's right,' Mrs Oates is right interjected Mrs Gale another neighbour. 'I have the address somewhere. Inspector, is the boy all right?'

'He's fine.'

'Mrs Gale, can you give the address to the sergeant?'

'We have no reason to come tomorrow, for this is your patch. We will leave it to you and your staff. I have contacted your superintendent, and he is on his way and over there are some more people who wish to give evidence. Before we leave, have you done all that is required doing photographs, fingerprints, etc.? Your super is a stickler for detail. We've done a few jobs together when I worked up here as a constable many years ago.'

The superintendent arrived and immediately took charge.

'Social Services, that's you,' remarked the superintendent. 'Now what will you do?'

'We take the boy into care.'

'You have had him in care once if not twice, and look what has happened.'

'I don't think so, not until we have our say. 'You've made a mess of this. You have tormented and tortured and almost ruined a young boy's life.'

'We have not Inspector. We are not to blame.'

'Well, who do we blame? I hope you are made to answer for what has happened.'

'Why blame us or me?'

I interjected 'It's you, Social Services your department, your people, your system. Don't give us that rubbish about being under pressure, understaffed, underpaid. There will be an investigation and a hearing about all this, and I'll be ready to say my piece.'

'That is fine, Mr Black, but what would you have done? We cannot be with them twenty-four hours a day.'

'Look, these people are druggies, a house of ill repute, and probably, it's the same with the one at the coast and the money they got off the State they used to run such operations. No, you will never convince me. It is you people who have failed in your job, full stop.'

'Henry is the one who has suffered, maybe for rest of his life. The finger points at you because it is you people who will have to answer, and if it was not for gypsies at Newark, that boy could have died in similar circumstances as he was found in a hedge bottom the day he was born. We have the gypsy fraternity to thank for that.'

'What do you mean, Mr Black?'

'What I say. Some day you may know but not today. Right now, we have Henry to think about, not you people. You can't be trusted. That lad wants caring for and loving, something he knows little about. Now shut up. You make my blood boil. I had a saying it was "blinking heck" to avoid swearing, and my god, I'm ready to let it rip.'

'Jimmy, that is enough. Now calm down. We'll sort it out later.'

'I know, Ken, but I'm so annoyed. How could such things happen?'

'Jimmy, give it a rest for now. There will be a hearing, and the truth will come out. Right now it is the boy and what ought to be done?'

'I tell you this, Ken, if you put him in a care home, he'll run away. What would you do? If you were him and gone through what he has gone through? This is a very sad case and requires handling carefully, and I'm glad I'm not a police officer or a social worker. I'm beginning to think Henry ought to be told the truth. We ought to discuss this. It may eliminate some pain.'

'What is the truth, Jimmy?'

'Not many know the truth. Sergeant, you know, what do you think?'

'I'm beginning to think the same as you, but we have to think of the child. It's his life and future but not for him to decide. I think it ought to be decided along with other matters.'

CHAPTER 5

Causes, Not the System

'HENRY, THESE PEOPLE wish to speak to you.'

'Grandad, I'm not going back there.'

'No, Henry, you are not.'

'I want to stay with you.'

'Henry, I want you too, but I don't think they'll allow it. You have to go with them.'

'Where will they take me grandad?'

'To a care home far side of town with other people around your age group, and at weekends you can come and visit me or I can come to you.'

'No! No! No, I'm not going. I'll run away. Everyone is cruel to me. Those who want me cannot have me, and those who I have been with have nearly killed me. Why can't I choose who to live with? No you're coming with us. Come now, we are the Social Services. It's our job to care for you and see you have the best we can provide.'

Henry yelled 'get your hands off me best you can provide you're a joke. You don't know what you're doing to me.'

'Mr Black, it's not our fault. It's the causes, not the system. The people he was with were sick people. They were not like that when Henry went to them.'

'No, it's a good thing that adoption wasn't carried out, but in two more months, I understand it may have. The boy is frightened and in fear of the system and the causes. The boy deserves better. How do you know you can provide that? You make judgements, and we hope to God you are right?'

'Mr Black, we've heard enough. He comes with us.'

'Well, I shall run away, no matter where you take me.'

'Mr Black, we have our job to do, and it's not easy. I am a senior social worker and agree with you, but I have to do my job, no matter how ugly it appears. We are trained officers and have to work by guidelines of what the State lays down. Things do go wrong from time to time. We don't always get things right. That percentage we get wrong is very small in comparison to the overall total. You talk about causes and systems. We have a system directed to us to follow from the highest level of the executives of the Civil Service. The causes are not our fault, and there are many. We can only act within the system provided and the guidelines.'

'Inspector, I am senior social worker could we speak in private? Henry will be fine with Mr Black, and sergeant and Hazel, the social worker. Henry looked frightened. What are they going to do to me grandad? Don't worry, my boy. They'll sort something out to suit us all.'

After about forty-five minutes, they all appeared with smiles and a look of satisfaction.

'Henry, what do you think about staying with Mr and Mrs Charles just down the road and go to school here?'

'I want to stay with you, grandad.'

'Henry, listen to me. You can call me grandad you can come here as often as you like, and you'll only be a street away.'

'Mr and Mrs Charles, I know them and like them can I stay with them?

'Henry, they have been vetted by Social Services and they have been waiting for some time to care for someone. We have sent for them to talk to you. Henry, your grandad has no wife as you know and is a little too old. Yes, we agree he is capable, but we think at this stage of life a couple would serve the purpose better.'

'Can I come and see you, Grandad?'

'Henry, I'll be upset if you don't.'

'Grandad, do you know Mr and Mrs Charles?'

'Yes. Violet went to school with Jenny, and they go shopping together.'

'Do you think they'll take me sometimes?'

'Of course, we will!' A voice was heard from the doorway; it was Violet's, Mrs Charles's.

'Henry, what do you think of that?'

'Grandad, I don't mind now. I feel happy and have not felt like this for years. Can I keep calling you grandad and Auntie Jenny?'

'Henry, we a have party on Saturday for your return.'

Then Henry threw himself at me, and we hugged; then he clasped Mrs Charles's hand as if he would never let go, looked up at the inspector and social care officers, and said thank you.

'We will see you tomorrow about ten, if you please, just a little paperwork, Mrs Charles.'

Then Henry danced down the garden path, holding hands with Violet. He turned just slightly, waved, and shouted, 'Love you, Grandad.'

Henry settled in and became very popular at school. He was well liked and became the captain of school cricket team at junior level. How pleased I was for when talking about sport, it was always cricket. I had won two medals playing cricket at school level and always pleased to talk about them. But what annoyed me most was at school cricket many boys who got chosen to play were not good enough but could get their sums right, or teachers knew very little about cricket and had their favourites.

Henry was growing fast and was happy with his surroundings. One day he approached me and asked, 'Why do people call me Blink?'

I was startled. 'Who calls you Blink?'

'Lots of boys I really don't mind. We all have nicknames, but mine is as if I'm blinking a lot.'

'Henry that's not the reason.'

'Well, what is the reason? Grandad, who were my real Mum and Dad? I know wherever I have lived, they're not my true Mum and Dad, but I think you know.'

'Henry, you'll be leaving school in a year or two and I think you ought to know, but I require the nod from other people.'

'You mean the Social Services, grandad?'

'Yes, I do.'

After a few days, Henry was back. 'Grandad, are my parents dead? You'll not hurt my feelings. I just wish to know. If they are not, I wish not to see them or contact them but would like to know. Before I forget, I've been chosen to join the Cricket Academy.'

'Good, my boy.'

'Come on, Grandad.'

'Henry, I wish not to upset you.'

'Grandad, it's time I ought to know.'

'Your parents fell sick. Your mum suffered from an incurable medical problem. There is name for it, but I can't pronounce it. She was giving birth to you, and it speeded up her illness. Your dad, he was heartbroken. He died with your mum in a stationary car with engine running. They became overcome with fumes. Ray and I were there, gathering chestnuts. They knew we were there, and placed you nearby for us to find you. You were only a few hours old. They meant us to take care of you. They must have known. Henry, when one is sick and dying, the mind plays strange things. I tell you this, they were good people.'

'How do you know I am that baby i?'

'Easy! You have a birthmark under your left arm as big as a fifty-pence piece. Your parents, I knew them well. Your dad was a good cricketer. I remember how he batted with style. His cover drives were a picture to see, a fine cricketer and sportsman. Your mother was pretty as a picture, and most appreciated with her many friends. Henry, now you know.'

'Thank you grandad I'll not cry but will remember what you have said for the rest of my life. They gave theirs in order for me to live. I'm not hurt. I feel proud. What about my name grandad?'

'Henry, I swore a lot when things didn't suit me. To stop me from swearing I would say "blinking heck". I don't know what it means, just a bit of slang that creeps into our vocabulary. Ray gave you that because it was first words I said when you were found. Your name "Henry" was found attached to you, and I'm your godfather.'

'Yes, and my grandad!' Then he threw his arms around me. We embraced with heavy throats. He mumbled, 'Thank you, Grandad! I love you and always will.'

CHAPTER 6

Schooling Days Are Over

HENRY WAS WELL settled with his new family and was happy. Now three years on, he was beginning to think about leaving school. He wondered what to do and looked for some independence. He called upon me for advice.

'Henry, what are you good at? What do you wish to do and why? Answer those questions, then you'll will be halfway there.'

'I like cricket, grandad. I want to play cricket.'

'You require a job to bring in an income right now. Keep your cricket going, even across winter, keep at it. I believe you can make it, but for a year or two we can find you a job at our garage and workshops. Jenny is coming around tonight, but Joe deals with that side of things. I'll have a word with them.'

'OK, thank you, grandad.'

'Hello, Ray, just saying how Henry is growing and Joe is thinking about a job for him when he leaves school.'

'That sounds fine Dad. I hear he's coming along nicely at cricket. What I wish to do over the winter period is give him some exercises to do. Bodybuilding, mind conditioning, and dietary and fitness programmes, so you Henry can join the course in November. I'll waive the fee this time for I hear you are being considered for Yorkshire Colts Cricket Club and I'm the physiotherapist for them. Thank you Ray. Henry to be selected, you must practise over winter in the indoor school.'

'Grandad, is that right?'

'Henry, my boy, you keep your nose clean and head down and work at it. You'll be fine.'

'Grandad, that's terrific. Thank you.'

'It's Ray to thank.'

'Well, thank you both.'

After tea, Jenny and Joe arrived. Henry had gone home. Joe mentioned that he is always ready to help. 'But we have a problem.'

'What do you mean, Joe?'

'It's like this. Yesterday at school during lunchtime, from the General Store of Mr Omar Youssef, three boys stole a large quantity of cigarettes and ran off. According to Mr Youssef, one of the boys was Henry. We are calling upon him later. We have spoken to him once. He says he was not there. Other two boys are saying nothing. Their dads have told them to say nothing.'

'Joe, may I speak to him?'

'Well, you'll have to ask Mr and Mrs Charles, not me.'

'Mr Charles, we have trouble with Henry. A circumstance has occurred whereas Henry is accused of stealing cigarettes with two more boys in their lunchtime at school. Henry says he wasn't there. It's not him, but the shop owner has identified him and others. Where is Mrs Charles?'

'She is upstairs with Henry. He is crying his eyes out saying no one believes him. He says those boys are lying. He wasn't there.'

'Will he come down? I wish to have a word.'

'I'll see. Henry, Mr Black and Sergeant Joe wish to speak to you.'

Henry came down and ran to me for some love.

'Here, here, now, Henry, you are a big boy now. Why did you steal cigarettes?'

'I didn't.'

'You did. I wish to know why you were in the shop tucking packets of cigarettes under your coat. Why did you do it? You stole to make yourself feel big in front of your so-called pals. You did it. Admit it you did it.'

'I didn't, Grandad.'

Henry was heartbroken. I was holding my hand up to stop others from interrupting and stared hard into Henry's face.

'You are a thief. You are nothing but a thief. Why did you do it?'

'I am not. I didn't do it,' Henry screamed and cried and cried.

'Mrs Charles, do you think we can have a drink please? And I think this young man would like a glass of orange.'

'Grandad, I didn't do it.'

'Henry, my boy, I know you didn't. You are perfectly innocent.'

Joe smiled. 'I think your grandad is right. Well done, Jimmy. Where did you learn that?'

'You are going to get married to my Jenny. She'll teach you a few things before you are much older.' That brought smiles and laughter, and they began to relax and enjoy each other's company.

'Jimmy, I have to make a report out for Mr Youssef wishes to bring prosecutions.'

'Right, Joe. Am I right to think this happened at 1 p.m. yesterday? You detained two boys at school and found packets of cigarettes in Henry's coat in the cloakroom. Am I right?'

'Correct.'

'And later, you questioned Henry after three o'clock, right?'

'Yes.'

'Mr Charles, what day was it yesterday?'

'It was Tuesday, yes and dentist day for Henry. I took him from school at midday, and we got back a little before three. Henry left his coat at school and retrieved it when he got back, so someone took Henry's coat across dinner time and returned it at about 1 p. m. So who is the third person? They thought to hide some cigarettes in Henry's coat, hoping they could get out of school before Henry and get the cigarettes. I ask you, those two boys, why do they lie? I wonder why.'

'Henry, who's the school bully?'

'That will be Billy Tuft. He once tried it on with me, but I thumped him. He only picks on small boys, and yes, you've got it. Those two are small.'

'And who smokes in the toilets at school? Who sells cigarettes at school? We have the picture, Henry.'

Changing subject, I said, 'Henry, I hear you have gained a place at winter nets for Yorkshire Colts Cricket Club.'

'I have?'

'Hooops! Sorry, did you not know?'

'Grandad, is that true?'

'Henry, we don't tell lies. We are always honest with each other, you know that.'

'I do now, Grandad.'

Next day, I informed Henry, 'You have a job at the garage when you leave school on the condition you follow Ray's instructions in keeping fit and healthy.'

'Thank you. I will. What will happen to the three who stole the cigarettes?'

'Two of them may have to go to another school, for it's not their first offence and they are very disruptive in school classes. As for the other one, he was bullied into doing what he did and comes from a home that could do better towards their children. A case that requires examination of parenthood and home family life, and constant assessment will be enforced. As for Mr Youssef, you all look alike to him. He admits he could have made a mistake.'

'Grandad, some people don't know when they're well off. For Christmas, Mr and Mrs Charles are buying me a cricket bat. When I get to the park, will you send a few balls down to me? I hear you were a fair left arm medium-pace spinner?'

'Henry, we will, and Joe is a fast bowler and pretty good, not good enough for county but good enough for council cricket. You'll get fast, medium, and spinners hurled down on you. By the beginning of next season, you'll be well tuned up. We'll see to that.'

'I'll want some protective gear: pads, gloves, helmet, arm bands, boots.'

'Henry, you'll be earning. Buy your own.'

'I will, Grandad!'

Then I grabbed him. 'You little devil! You know full well we'll take care of you'! And I gave him a great big hug.

'Mr Charles how is Henry with you? Jimmy, that boy is coming on in leaps and bounds – a fast learner, and we are proud to have him under our roof. Not a bit of trouble. Mrs Charles will miss him when the time comes. Does he know about his real Mum and Dad?'

'Yes, I did tell him. He took it well. You don't mind, do you?'

'No. We just wondered. I think it's best.'

'I hope he learns fast when he works in the garage. He can tinker with my car at weekends, because that's all I seem to do. Then it's soon Monday again. It doesn't seem long when Blink was a baby, and now he is ready for leaving school.'

'Grandad, when I start earning, would it be a good idea if I open a bank account?'

'Thought you had Henry.'

'I may not have much to save, but what I have, I will save for later in life. You see, Grandad, I don't wish to be without. I wish not to rely on others. It's my life, and I wish to take care of it. Being born into a situation like mine makes me think. I have no problems with Mr and Mrs Charles – wonderful people, and I couldn't thank them enough. But time is near for me to be thinking about me, not in a selfish way, but what to do with my life. Grandad, will you help me?'

'Henry, Mr and Mrs Charles have just heard you. Did you wish for them to hear you?'

Mr Charles interjected, 'We all will help you. Now go to bed.'

CHAPTER 7

Too Much Pain, Not Enough Pleasure

WORK AT THE garage was ideal. Henry was learning to drive, and I called a couple a times during the week on my walkabouts. I'm not a motorist. I'm a walker, and very often I would walk several miles before lunch. It was whilst I was out walking that I heard voices of coming through. It was the rambling group with their packs on their backs and big boots. Their bulky socks were tucked into trouser bottoms, and they were rambling at a speed faster than I could run. I stood aside and let them through as I could be in their way. They acknowledged me in a most socialistic manner, strange really. I liked their approach and laughed, saying, 'They are like a Christmas card, always greeting.'

'Henry, you know that rambling group I see? There is a blue-eyed lass who keeps enquiring about you, what are you up to?'

'Grandad, it's Margaret. You know them. They call to fill up, and I put their car through for a wash. Her dad always tips me. That's them with the Rover.'

'And that's Bob, the bouncer.'

'What, Grandad?'

'Bob, captain of our cricket team. Anyway, she is taking a shine to you, and you are only sixteen. I had to wait till I was twenty-five.'

'Well, Grandad, Ray thinks I ought to get involved in rambling keep me fit and healthy.'

One day, as Henry was giving a car a polish he noticed something strange on the rear seat of the car – a woman's handbag and two gents' wallets. He took the car number; they paid with a large tip. He informed Jenny, who phoned Joe at the police station. The car was stopped several miles away. Apparently, they had been to the races and had been doing a lot of pickpocketing or lifting anything that could be lifted. There were others involved. It was a large gang operating all over the racing fraternity. According to Joe, the following Saturday, there was to be another race meeting. The fair people were already arriving and assembling their fixtures to open on Friday night at 6 p.m., and Joe would be there with another constable to see if they could get the gang. Henry was asked if he cared to go to see if he recognised anyone who may have called at the garage and had forgotten to pay for petrol; they were on CCTV, and Joe thought it could be same gang.

Henry thought, 'I'll take Margaret to the fair if I have courage enough to ask.' He had, and Margaret was overjoyed.

'See you at six thirty then.'

'That was it,' thought Henry. But other boys who fancied going out with Margaret became jealous. Henry was getting warning signs from others but tried to ignore it for these are the few who stand about at street corners with a can of beer and a fag, not knowing what to do, giving the impression of being bored and blaming everyone apart from themselves.

On Friday night, Henry and Margaret prepared to enjoy themselves at the racecourse ground fair. Whilst they enjoyed themselves on the carousel and rides that go up and down or round and round, Joe and a constable in plain clothes walked in opposite directions around the ground. It was whilst having a cola and hot dog that someone shouted, 'Henry.' He turned to see gypsy Rose Knowles, who had nursed him when he was lost in the forest at Newark. She was sitting at her open-door caravan, anticipating anyone wishing to have their palms read.

'Is that you, Henry?' Rose asked.

'Rose! Hello, how are you? I have often thought of you.'

'And I of you come in, Henry.'

'Rose, this is Margaret.'

'Please be seated.'

'Rose, you're not going to tell me my fortune?'

'Henry, I did that many years ago. Am I right so far? I can tell Margaret hers. Would you like that, my dear?'

'Rose, how is Nick? I have often thought about him finding me in the woods.'

'Nick is in custody at the police station, accused of stealing a white van and scrap metal and copper wire from railway property.'

'Rose, did he do it?'

'You know better than to ask me that. What you expect me to say? We are gypsies. The public look upon us as outcasts because our way of life is different from theirs. They say we don't pay our road tax, we don't let our children go to school, we steal, we are dirty, we ransack property that local authorities provide. Yes, a lot of their comments are through ignorance and misunderstanding of what it is. We have not moved with the times, for they were like us many years ago when much land was forestry and there were no manufacturing industries. People changed with time. We refused and are dammed for being what we are.

'We are tormented, insulted, spat at, denied some rights, blamed for what others do, accused of being thieves and troublemakers, not allowed into various buildings and establishments, and yet people come to me and wish for their fortunes to be told – selfish, greedy devils.'

'Rose, steady on.'

'Well, some people make me sick. They say we are lazy and do not pay our way. I can point to almost two million people who don't work. The prisons are full but not of gypsies. We don't sign on unemployment and you don't see us hanging about dole offices. We don't condemn you for what you do. Why should we be condemned? We refuse to be conditioned, a right we have. Many people would do better if they protected their rights instead of criticising others. Henry, sorry, I'm going on. Now, my dear,' she said, looking at Margret, 'you'll have some good luck and bad. You could lose someone or thing very close to you, maybe an animal, a dog or something that you love. How do I know that you may ask I see your eyes you cry a lot, but you'll have a long, happy life and travel a lot.'

Later, while walking around the fairground, Henry noticed the two who had called at the garage and left without paying. He pointed them out to Joe, who apprehended them. Upon searching them, Joe found drugs on them; then he arrested them for being in possession of illegal drugs. He could see an occurrence arising and called for back-up. On their arrival, both were bundled into the police van. Joe mentioned to one of them, 'You are arrested for the theft of cable and a white van and stealing petrol. You could go down for a long time. Your friend says it was you that stole van and cable. He is wishing you to take the rap, and you broke into school and stole some tools from the woodworking classroom. Make it easy on yourself. You're not a bad lad. I know your dad well.'

'Sergeant, it was Roddy. He stole the van and the cable and put it in a field at the back of a haystack to pick up later. It's down Lovers Lane, about halfway down. Look left at back of that haystack.'

'Who blamed others for stealing?'

'That was Roddy. He got us to blame the gypsies.'

'Us you say "us"? Who are the others?'

'Fred Simms, and Viv Doon.'

'Thank you. I'll have a word with your Dad and see what we can do.' Joe then whispered to his constable, and later, Nick was released from custody and reunited with his family. Upon seeing Henry, he gave him an almighty hug. It prompted Henry to say, 'Blinking heck! You're hurting me, you great big bear! How are you?'

Nick, with his red-and-gold-coloured neckerchief and checked thick striped shirt with cord trousers and big brown boots was always a spectacle to see – a most impressive man with lots of charm and good looks.

'We are moving on tomorrow, Henry. We go north for two months. We are always pleased to see you, but it's getting late and you have to go now. The coppers have taken up a lot of my time, but I had a nice breakfast and tomato soup for dinner with a bread bun. Nobody seems to eat rabbit soup any more. Henry, I've a conference in a few weeks, a gypsy conference. The agenda will be the same as last year, always about rights to land and settlements. It's getting more difficult every year with acts laid down that go back hundreds of years. We have great knowledge in researching such things and surprise many in courts, whom we have to challenge for our rights. So, Henry, put your hand to mine, and I bid you both good luck.'

Margaret was so surprised and told her Dad who commented, 'Gypsies can lead a difficult life. They follow their customs. Who are we to judge when we have a crime rate like we do? I don't see many gypsy children in care, and their parents in prison. What I do see is a lot of dissent from some people who should know better. You see, Margaret, if I'm annoyed with someone, I curse them. If gypsies curse someone, they could be prosecuted. We have to try and understand all points of view before we condemn. We seek pleasure rather than pain. We seek comfort as against discomfort and peace rather than war. We should help rather than ignore and do what is best for the majority, but most of all, if you wish to judge, be prepared to be judged yourself.'

'Dad, I know you are a Methodist preacher, but today isn't Sunday.'

'Margaret, you'll do well to listen and read more.'

CHAPTER 8

The Love Ones

HENRY WAS SEEING more of Margaret. They seemed very happy together. Henry was now looking towards his driving test and saving his tips. He got to thinking about what to do with his life beyond cricket if he was not good enough. He asked me. I snarled, 'Get that out of your head! Don't have doubts. Ray, tell me how things are with Henry? He's been working very hard in practice, and from last year has made good progress. Well, he seems a little down with himself.'

'Yes. That is because I'm working him hard. In the next four or five weeks, it will get easier. I warned him when we started it would get tough, but them he doesn't complain. Has he to you?'

'No, but he seems unsettled. I know what it is. He's in love.'

I was doing a bit of pruning to my roses when I heard 'Hello, Jimmy!' It was the county coach for cricket Fred Parr. Thought I'd give you a call. Jimmy. It's about Henry. We've been watching him through the winter months. His fitness is great, his bowling is good, but I'm afraid his batting is . . . '

'No! Don't tell me!'

'I have to tell you, Jimmy. His batting is excellent, and he has been selected for the second squad. If he does well, in which I think he will, he could get into first squad eleven. We have at least a couple who'll be selected for the test series. Then Henry will have his opportunity. I leave you this letter of confirmation. Tells you all you require to know, and, Jimmy, we are dealing with you. What about Mr and Mrs Charles?'

'That's all right. They are aware of what we are doing and will be overjoyed. Tell you what, I'll give them a ring now whilst you are here Fred and you can speak to them. Thanks Jimmy.

Mr. Charles took the call and was overjoyed and to hear first cricket match in May at home at Scarborough, against Nottinghamshire. Mr Charles informed Ray, then Ray sought Henry out and warned him not to let up on his training there is three more weeks of fitness training to go. I know you are seeing Margaret, but don't neglect your new-found fame it's your driving test next week. If you pass, you can have that car you have been working on for the last four weeks. But if you go cricketing, I'm going to lose you. Maybe I may get the tips you have been getting. Henry, you know we wish you well, and I wish to sign your bat before any runs are knocked off it.'

Henry informed Margret, who was rather quiet during their rambling.

'What is it Margret?'

'Henry, it's Mum. She has cancer. She goes for more tests next week, but it's serious. Doctors have warned Dad to expect the worst.'

'Margret, I'm so sorry.'

'Henry, they say four or five weeks at most. I had plans to go to university, but not now my heart is not in it. If anything, I wish to marry you in two or three years.'

'Thank you, Margaret. Do I have a say in any of this?'

'Henry, look at those people looking at us. Have we been speaking loudly for a few heads have been turning. Say no more until we get to the cafe for a break from rambling.'

Almost to the day, Margaret's Mum died. It was a very sad occasion; many attended the funeral for she was well respected and loved especially for her help to the WVS and charity work for the underprivileged children. Henry, thought, 'This is the very woman that helped me when I was so young, and I didn't know. But she knew. No wonder she would enquire about me and ask how things are with me.' Henry thought long and hard about his upbringing in the past and asked Mr and Mrs Charles, 'Did Margaret's Mum do anything in you taking care of me?'

'Henry, for you she was an angel. You see, she would have loved to have a son. It was not to be, but it was through her that we became your guardians.'

'Thank you for that for I'm grateful to you for giving me a good childhood.'

Margaret now withdrew from her plans to go to university and thought, 'A job with sufficient income will do, for Dad needs me close to him. Connie has offered me a job in the Bakery and Bread shop. I'm taking it. Only trouble is, Henry, you play cricket on Saturday. It'll be difficult to get away from the shop on Saturdays.'

Henry gave her the good news, and she gave Henry hers with much laughter.

'We will sort something out. Let us just be grateful for the time being for what we have.'

'Margaret, you talked about marriage. I would prefer to wait until I'm twenty-one. Then have some security behind me. I might not make it at cricket. Then what? If I do, there will be a lot of travelling involved, and we could be away from each other for some time. You may not like it. You may meet someone else, or I too.'

'Stop it! Henry, don't talk like that. If you want it to happen, it will. Do you wish for that?'

'Of course not!'

'Well, don't say such things. People are looking again and heads are turning, so change the subject.'

A woman walked by and tapped Henry on shoulder and said, 'That has told you, young man!' Both looked at each other and laughed.

'What concerns me, Henry, is what surname do you use?'

'Pleased you ask that. No one seems to be concerned I'm only Henry to many and use the name "Bloom". I will see grandad. I don't know of a birth certificate. Mr Charles may know.'

At tea, Henry asked Mrs Charles the question. 'What have you been using?'

'Bloom.'

'And that's what's on your birth certificate, and I have it right here.'

'What is it? Does that give you concern?'

'No, that's fine. Well, you can have it changed if you wish.'

'No, it's fine. Well, I plan to marry when I'm twenty-one and that's the name I've been using, but it was just a thought.'

'Henry, we don't mind. It's not the name. It's you yourself that matters, and you have made us proud of you.'

Love life blossomed for Henry and Margaret. They went to church together to hear her Dad's sermons, who sometimes affixed his eyes on them as if he was only talking to them. But he liked Henry a lot and loved for Henry to walk around church grounds with him, discussing topics of the day and slipping in odd tips of advice – not of Christianity, not of rights and wrongs, not of politics of the day, but of cricket, his second religion. He would say, 'Vitai Lampada (The torch of life).' It's a well-known saying 'Play up, play up, and play the game' from a book of poems by Sir Henry Newbolt (6 June 1862 to 19 April 1938). He thrust it into Henry's chest. 'Read that, my son, then read this *Wisden Cricketers' Almanack* and who is who in the cricketing world. Remember this, you will have many knocks in life, but your greatest knocks are to be on the cricket fields. So prepare yourself to "play up, play up, and play the game" on those rich green, green fields of England, where battles are fought and won.

'I tell you something, Henry. Many say football is our national game. It's a greater spectator sport. I think King James the First outlawed it as a game for ruffians and "cricket for gentlemen". I believe cricket be our national game. Football, as far as I know, has never been withdrawn from King James' ruling. To be honest, we have two national sports, football and cricket, one for winter and one for summer. No matter what arguments, it's how the game is played. Be a sport, be a player, play up, and play the game. So ends my sermon for today. I wish you good luck. Godspeed! For me you are playing best game in the world. I think I give better sermons out of the church than in it.' Both laughed and turned to each other. Henry stuck his hand out to say thank you; Margaret's Dad took Henry's hand in both of his hands and squeezed it hard. 'Good luck, my boy and godspeed.'

CHAPTER 9

Not All Fun and Games

'HENRY BLOOM', THE name on the driving license. Now I am eighteen. With another good season of cricket behind me, averaging forty-five with bat, I was chosen to tour with England. 'Margaret, this is what I mean. We are going to be apart for some time. This is my job. I have a contract and have worked hard for it. The downside to it is we'll be apart.'

'Henry, we have discussed this, and you have to get on with it. I'll be here when you get back.'

'Margaret, I don't want to lose you.'

'No fear of that. I'll be here when you get back. You have laptop and mobile phone. We'll contact each other every day and do send pictures. When you return at the end of the games, we'll make plans for the wedding. We'll be going on nineteen. It'll soon come around. You must not go overseas with domestic problems. Stay focused on your cricket.'

'Margaret, Jenny tells me at the garage people who haven't called before have been calling. She thinks it's of me. I must admit many ask for my autograph, good for business and serves me well. Are you all right at the bakery shop?'

'Why do you ask?'

'Jenny would like you to work at the garage when I go on the tour. The job is there if you want it. Have a word with Jenny if interested. Grandad would like you to take the job because it's a family concern. Joe, his job is policing as you know, with CID and can be called away at all hours.'

'Henry, I'll think about it because large retail shops are taking much of the sales away from small operators, and some have been forced to close down through loss of trade.'

'It's what people say, work hard, and play hard. Times I've heard that said, probably from many who done neither. We have certainly worked hard this last year. We deserve a break but not yet, but we can go to the capital at weekend for a day. I wish to buy you an engagement ring.'

Margaret threw her arms around Henry. 'It's my Saturday off this week.'

'I know. I've checked. When cricket starts again, there will not be any Saturdays off, so let's take advantage of it. On Sunday, we have a party laid on at Cricketers Arms and your shop is doing the catering. That's something else you didn't know.'

Saturday in the capital, Margaret was excited, picking and choosing a ring, picking them up and putting them down – spoilt for choice. It was 'take your time. You only do it once.'

'What about this one?' an inpatient assistant asked, flicking his hands in the air, forcing his white shirt cuffs to be prominent from his coat. 'Madam, it's lovely on you!'

'Henry, what do you think?' Margaret asked, holding her hand out and clenching the box that carried price tag with the other.

'Margaret, if you want it, then it's yours.'

'I'll take it please.'

'Thank you. Shall I pack it, madam?'

'No! It is on and there it stays.'

Henry approached the till to pay, and upon paying was informed that there was a 25 per cent discount. Acknowledging it, Henry answered, 'I know,' and a little smile became noticeable upon the assistant's face.

'Will there be anything else, sir?'

'Yes. That handbag she was looking at earlier. Wrap it. I wish her not to see it.'

'Sir, we have coffee machine over there. If you distract her to it, she'll not see me wrap it.'

Later, they called for lunch, and Margaret was inquisitive about the parcel. Henry placed it in front of her. 'It's for you.'

She opened it, and how she marvelled at the designer handbag! Henry assisted her in opening it and, unseen by Margret, slipped a five-pound note into it. When she discovered it, he explained, 'A superstition of you'll never be without money. Nick, you know you had your fortune told by his mother? He told me that.'

'Henry, what his mum said to me has come true. She said other things, but I'm not speaking of them.'

'What was that?'

'Wait and see!'

'Steady on, Margaret. We have another eighteen months before we marry.'

'Henry, when we get home, the fair will be back on recreation ground. I noticed them arriving. Wonder if Nick and his mum are with then? I've forgotten her name, but remember what she says.'

'It is Rose Knowles. Well, I think I'll give her another call.'

On entering the site, Henry asked a young boy, 'Which is Mrs Knowles and Nick's van?'

'Are you the undertaker, mister?'

'Why? Who has died?'

'Nick mister. That's their van, the white one.' Then Rose saw them and greeted them, inviting them into her van amongst some of her friends.

Nick was in Cart Wheel pub; he wasn't even involved in a fight. Someone threw a glass from the bar right across the room. Two men started to fight; then people tried to leave. That was when Nick received stab wounds. Many had been witness to the incident. Then a police car pulled up at the caravan. It was Joe. 'Mrs Knowles, we have arrested three men. They are assisting us with our enquiries. Cannot say much more, but to say we are sorry and can we help in any way? And we'll keep you informed of any further developments.'

Joe continued, 'Henry, can I have a word? We have arrested Roddy Gere, Fred Simms, and Viv Doon, who got done for nicking petrol. Wouldn't take warnings or whatever they got and now it's murder. All is on CCTV. They caused a fight saying they hate gypsies 'and all gypsies should be kicked out'. The bar-keeper said, "I'll serve who I wish. If you're unhappy, go elsewhere." And that Roddy said, "If you don't, I will," and someone tried to stop him. So he swung a punch, broke loose, and stabbed Nick, who died on his way to hospital. I say enquiries are continuing, but really that's it.'

The funeral was attended by hundreds; roads closed to traffic to allow a large procession to take place of people from across the land, from north and south, east and west – the gypsy fraternity showing their support for Rose and respects to Nick. It was a show of companionship, the bringing together of kinsfolk, to say goodbye to one of their own. Tributes received were worthy of nobility, and perhaps he was, for those who condemn such people and their way of life ought to learn how to give respect to the dead.

Gypsies' journey through life is full of close-knitted companions and clansman-ships; you can see some of the most beautiful caravans that could take your breath away. As Henry laid the wreath, he thought, 'I've lost a friend who saved my life, a dear friend who received no glory only undeserved blame from an ignorant few. Goodbye, my friend, God bless.'

Henry was very much disturbed and found it hard to come to terms with the loss of his friend. Rose was preparing to move on to another site further south, where her other son, Denny, and his wife live. 'Henry, I wish you to have this bead with many charms on it. Nick liked to think it was lucky. He was not wearing it at the time and this clip-ring, it's to hold one's neckerchief together. It is silver.'

'Rose, I'm going to miss you. If or when you are up this way again, call on us.'

'Henry, thank you. Maybe next spring, for winter is setting in fast. So I'll say, take care, and may luck be with you.'

The postman called with a letter, and Henry was chosen for the winter tour of South Africa with the MCC, and he was only eighteen and a half years old. 'Margaret, I go first week in December, so this is a testing time for it's what we have discussed and prepared for. Will you be all right?'

'Yes. You go. Your grandad and my Dad will see to that. I start at garage next Monday. Bakery /Bread shop is closing down. Superstores are taking the trade away from small shops, but Jenny is thrilled to bits for me to join her. Henry, you go for your cricket. We are all proud of you. I've started an album of your photos and cuttings. When we're old and grey, we can look back with fond memories.'

'Yes, Margaret, we can, but I know Grandad is not in good health and I worry sometimes.'

'Henry, don't let him know that. Your mind must be focused on cricket. We'll take care of him. There'll not be many goods sold by him at the garage. He'll be tied to the TV, watching you. Don't worry, Henry, for if he knows, you'll upset him. Now go round and give him the good news.'

CHAPTER 10

South Africa

'GRANDAD WAS OVERWHELMED with the news he looked hard at me then said. Blink, you've made me proud. We have watched and encouraged you. Ray put you through it so to speak, and you never grumbled or moaned or dodged your responsibilities. You deserve credit for that. Now the hard work is done in your fitness. Don't let it slip. You must maintain fitness and keep your body healthy. You are a lucky young man with immense talent. Don't throw it away.'

'Grandad, I would hate to let you down because it's you and Mr Charles who pushed a bat in my hand many years ago. You mentioned I'm an awkward devil being left-handed, and I kept calling you Grandad and you would say "I'm not your Grandad". You don't say that now.'

'Henry, I am so happy. Thank you for that. Do remember and play up, and play the game and keep me informed on that lap top and e-mail of what is happening in detail.'

My first e – mail read grandad, first game is coming up, and all have been doing well in friendly matches. It's now test matches against South Africa, only eleven can play and competition is strong. Grandad many sport writers say it's the strongest team ever sent out to South Africa and England expect good results we've had our talk from the captain and the selectors in what they expect – a few do's and don'ts. Then the team was selected. I'm third wicket down, and congratulations all around, especially from the older members of the team.

First game of the series, England is batting on a hard wicket, baked by the constant sun, but a wicket with runs in it. I was informed about the long hot playing hours, and was advised to have some suntan oil and salt tablets handy. Your tip grandad was 'keep a jar of honey in the kit bag and take a couple of spoonfuls a day, and I do.

Grandad wished to know every detail for his album he kept of me and he liked to think he was there so I e – mailed. The match opened, England was batting, and I went down to the boundary ropes to have a look at the deliveries and the bowlers who were sending them down over a hundred miles an hour. I thought, 'These look good. Might be tired when I get in, but then other bowlers are good. They're a good team all the way down the order.'

Openers were doing well, thirty off first eight overs – a steady start, playing to a packed house. These people really love their cricket. Two appeals turned down and the batsmen are on the back foot. Some good bowling from the openers, keeping the score down, but the fifty came up and the opener was caught behind for twenty-four. Then the score crept to eighty for one, when a mix-up in running in between wickets resulted in a silly run out. 'Henry,' said the captain, 'good luck. Just take your time and play your own game.' The first delivery whistled passed my head; next I played straight back to the bowler. Other two deliveries were unplayable.

Between the overs, my partner walked down wicket to me – now all the team call me Blink – and said, 'Watch him, Blink, just give him a straight bat and leave them alone outside off stump. He has four slips and a deep point. That's where he picks up most of his wickets.'

Two runs off the next over. I was facing the same bowler again. A ball down leg side, a gift, and I put it away for four runs; next delivery brought two runs through the covers, then one on leg side. Over called, then I faced the bowling and again a cover drive – a four, and so it went on, and I was out, caught for fifty-two. I had proved my point, and computers were flashing messages across the world.

Many discussions followed why the game was lost. There was not a lot to say; it was a tight game, a bowler's wicket, always favoured the side fielding first. No change for the next match which the MCC or England won by a similar margin – a seventy-four from me, and so it went on until the final game of the series. There was a capacity crowd to watch who wins and takes the series. South Africa, batting first on a good wicket, made 354 all out. England scored 350 in the first innings; South Africa scored 321 in second innings. England required 326 to win, and were 293 for 8. I was 89 not out and realised it was down to me for the tail-enders weren't expected to score many runs. We required 33 runs – four byes and a single, and over; 28 required, and I was probably facing the fastest bowler ever. First two deliveries flashed past my head, another went through to the keeper – a loud appeal, not out. Next one played and flew through the slips, dropped short for a catch but found the boundary; 24 required, a drive through the covers for 2, and then a one to face the bowling again.

I was on 96, and the end of game was in sight. There was an appeal of LBW; I was given 'not out'. A 2, now I was on 98, and then I put a shot through the covers – a delightful shot for four! The crowd went wild with joy. I held my bat high in appreciation, but the game was not over. Next delivery resulted in another four, and then a one; next deliveries were unplayable, and the over was called. Now 10 runs were required, and the batsman faced the hurricane. First two deliveries flew through to the wicketkeeper next two rattled him on the pads – loud appeals, not out. The fifth delivery splatted batsmans stumps. Now it was 10 to make and the last man in. Something came over me. I stood in silence and thought of Margaret's dad, and Sir Henry Newbolt, 'play up, and play the game'; one more ball for the new batsman to face – he blocked it, over called. I was to face the bowler, a 4, a 2, another 2; then 2 were required. A cover drive, a race to the boundary, a four, and it's all over. I was 119 not out; the series was won, and the crowd went wild, especially the 'Barmy Army' that is, English supporters who follow and support the team. Grandad texted back, well done my boy. I thought, grandad seen all this on his T.V. but liked to view his album cuttings and show to others.

I was man of the match; sport pages of newspapers were full of my innings. I was a hero to many, and schoolboys loved me. I was famous the cricketing world over. I was young and good-looking, which resulted in advertising and publishing various products. It was getting out of hand. I didn't wish to be distracted from my duties of an England player and decided to put all that business on to my grandad and Mr Charles, so anyone enquiring were given their contact numbers as they were my agents. I was thinking of taking things a little easy until the English cricket seasons started again. Whilst packing my bags to go home, I came across the silver neckerchief clip that Nick's Mum had given me for good luck. I kissed it and returned it to its place amongst my cricket clothing.

It was touchdown time at the airport, then home. On arriving home, I was greeted by many. Margaret threw her arms around me and then informed me that Grandad was in hospital and it was not too good.

'Henry, is that you, my boy? You've done well and made me proud. I always knew you had it in you.' Many coughs followed. 'I'm going to see you at Lords against the old enemy, Australians.'

'We'll get them Ashes back, Grandad.'

'You do that for me, my boy.'

'I promise, Grandad. I love you, Grandad. Grandad Grandad! Nurse! Nurse. That was end of play for Grandad.

Grandad was buried alongside his wife, Mable. I felt I had lost a part of myself and thought, 'This is going to be hard to overcome, but I must for Grandad would wish for me to keep on playing the game he so much loved and would say, "No matter what. Play up, play up, and play the game"'.

The turnout from the public gave testimony to his popularity; the cemetery was blanketed with flowers, a tribute most worthy of a lovely man. At the service, I paid tribute by reading a poem by Sir Henry Newbolt.

First Verse

Vitai Lampada
(The Torch of Life)

There's a breathless hush in the close tonight
Ten to make and the last man in
A bumping pitch and blinding light
An hour to play and the last man in
And it's not for the sake of a ribbon coat
Or a selfish hope of a seasons fame
But his captain's hands on his shoulder smote
Play up! Play up! Play the game.

Goodbye, Grandad
May God be with You
From your boy, Henry
'Blink'

CHAPTER II

Jennifer's Garage

A T THE GARAGE, Benny had taken up employment at the nearby electrical firm and Ethel had left the district, so Jennifer was pleased to know that Margaret had joined them. The concern was with just two women working or running the garage, it could prove to be difficult. What was required was a man. I was available only when I was not playing cricket. It was a family concern. There was no way the garage could be run twenty-four hours with the staff available. Jennifer thought it best to call a meeting of family to discuss the situation.

Ray was asked if he was still interested in the family garage now that Grandad was not with us. It was a yes. Jennifer said, 'Dad left instructions for everyone to be embraced in the family affairs, as one family. But Henry is away cricketing. Wait a minute, Ray. Henry is coming here to this meeting. I've invited him, so hang on before you start making suggestions for I've some things to report as being eldest family member. So let's deal with things in an orderly fashion.

'Henry, take a seat. Now we are all here, I wish to inform you I have received the report from the solicitors about Dad's will. I can report this to you, but we are required next week to present ourselves at his office for clarification upon what details I tell you today. The report goes on to say the garage to be a family concern with me as chairperson of the company called Jenny Blacks Garage and Workshops. Please hear me out. Margaret, when she marries, is also to be a committee member of the company.

'Our Dad left a considerable amount of money, sufficient to open up workshops for motor repairs, MOTs, and whatever a motorist requires for salesrooms. We have plenty of space. Joe informs me police transport will be giving us a contract for petrol and motor repairs. This will be ready in five weeks. Everything will be up and running by then. Joe has two mechanics who worked on police cars in mind for the place they had is being moved and some of the work is being transferred to us. You, Ray, say you are available now that you have taken a post with football team, and Henry, you are here when not away cricketing. We have to look more into it and see what we can sort out. We open 24/7, so more staff will be required, at least two. Every family member is to be a committee member responsible for different aspects of work within the company. We have a committee meeting once a month unless otherwise arranged. That's about it from me. You'll learn more next week about financial matters. Right now we are just getting the garage and workshops organised any questions?'

'Jennifer, the land behind the garage, Dad once told me it all belongs to us and he had planned at one time to build on it.'

'You are right, Ray. That's not accounted for in the plans for extension.'

'What I would like is to build a fitness centre on it not only for the football club – who have lost their premises – but also for the public. This would serve well with the garage and workshops and salerooms having all under one umbrella. Further to that, we have room to open a cafe for drivers and commercial use. I know it costs money, so I say if finances run to it, I propose this should be done.'

'It's a good idea, and I think we can do it. Let us see what the solicitor has to say next week. Henry, you are part of this, so what do you think?'

'I think we should utilise all spare land. I would like to see indoor sport training facilities like indoor practice nets for cricket, along with other sports. Land is not much good if we don't use it, and each department can have its own autonomous body. When I marry Margaret, we'll require somewhere to live. The rooms attached to the garage can be utilised as living accommodation, and we can live there. I think we ought to make full use of everything we have.'

'Henry, again good ideas, and if funds run to it, we'll do it. I'm not in favour of going into debt to achieve it, in case we fail. We only enter into business if we have success, no risks, only good financial sense, and Joe knows a good accountant.'

The solicitor called rather than us going to his office. His large briefcase was so fat and bulky, one would think he had brought all the companies' workload with him. He was such a funny-looking man with horn-rimmed glasses, far too large for a small man; in fact, all he wore was not fitting for a professional man. It was more suitable for a man down on his luck. Then he spoke in a way that demanded attention. Giving himself an introduction, he spoke fluently in short sharp sentences with pleasant smiles, giving a sense of friendliness with a cute twinkle in his eyes. Then he opened his briefcase, and a whole lot of paperwork escaped, looking for daylight. Did he care? Not one iota! It was 'tut, tut, tut', then he found the files that responded to the situation and there we were, down to business. He read the will:

'This is the will of Mr James Black. He leaves all property at the garage and the garage to the family, and that Henry be part of the family at all levels of business matters. All land has building permission and plans that are here with me for workshops for MOT and motor repairs, a cafe, and a fitness centre with living accommodation provided and attached to the garage. The old barn-cum-stables to be demolished and indoor sports facility to be built and indoor cricket practice nets established. Jennifer is head of the family and senior executive, whilst Henry is away playing cricket. The sports centre to be kept open throughout the year for indoor bowls, table tennis, basketball, and any other that can be accommodated. There are plans here and approved for a car valeting area, and that's it for that side of things.

'Money matters that you are more interested in on how will this be done?' Most of it is paid for, and money is held by us 'solicitors' for other projects. There will be £ 4,500 (four thousand five hundred pounds) for the cafe to be up and running. We estimate much less. Funds are available for indoor sports; £ 3,000 (three thousand pounds for workshops). In all, £7.000 (seven thousand pounds will more than cover everything). That leaves £200,000 (two hundred thousand pounds surplus). It goes on to say here that £ 100. 000 (one hundred thousand for working capital,) no less, at all times. For the family, that is about£20. 000 (twenty thousand pounds) each less my admin costs. I believe Jenny has briefed you in how the company is to a be run – the cafe to be named Jenny's Place, workshops known has Jenny's Workshops, indoor exercise and physiotherapy and sports and pastimes known as Jenny's Health and Care Centre.

'We have informed the contractors, and we accept that all work will be completed in five weeks. We, being solicitors, hold the deeds, and will assist in all business matters relating to any legal representation. If or when anyone wishes to hop out and leave the company and business matters relating to what I have said, they will be rewarded with twenty thousand pounds sterling. Only after five years, anyone not wishing to be part of business matters and decides to remain with the company, will receive twenty thousand pounds when five years has expired. If within company service and one violates their contract known as "industrial misconduct", they'll lose all benefits, but if after five years and one takes their twenty thousand pounds, the vacancy will be offered to other family members of a deposit of twenty thousand pounds or four payments of five thousand pounds over two years plus interest. Failure to pay on time stipulated disqualifies payee without redress.'

'That is my report of the will of Mr Black. There are a few more items you should know but they are not related to what has been said, mainly requests of which we discuss at a later stage. Anyone wish to ask questions that you may not understand or anything you are not clear with? Jenny, there you have it. I bid you all a good day and a prosperous future.'

CHAPTER 12

The Family

T HERE WERE A few surprises but no grumbles about the will. I had to make my point that I felt a little embarrassed at being included in the will as equal to all the family. I called him Grandad; many a time he would remind me that he was not my grandad, but I kept calling him that. 'Jenny, I'm missing him. He told me the story about finding me under a bush, and the rest I know. I was suffering in my childhood, and I think he saved my life on more than one occasion. And then he dies and leaves me to be a member of your family.'

'Henry, you are family and will be treated as such. What you should be doing is concentrate on your wedding plans. Henry, what I wish of you is the family must come first in all matters.'

'Thank you, Jenny, I will. My last guardians have been good to me and I took their name, but feel I ought to add the name "Black" to mine. Then I'll be more comfortable in representing the family. Jenny, be truthful with me. What do others think of me?'

'Henry, why don't you ask them? You're in because we wanted you in and so did our dad. Now can we forget it and get on with what we are good at? That is making money? We all have jobs to do. Now get on with it. Get your section or department and call it what you like. Get it sorted and up and running, for you'll be away cricketing. Make good your time, and you'll require someone to run it in your absence. You have plenty to think about for if you wish Margaret to run it, then she'll have to learn of what is required. She's fine with the garage. Maybe we leave her there, and you employ someone for the indoor games department and social activities.'

'Jenny, I think you are right. I'll give it a lot of thought. We've a few weeks to plan and organise, and when we are ready, we ought to call another meeting to put everyone in the picture.'

'Henry, we'll have a meeting once a month. Ray, how long have you been there listening?'

'I have heard all and agree. Henry, cut it out. You are one of us now. My job is health and fitness. We all work together and help each other if or when it's necessary. As Jenny says, we are a family first and foremost.

'Margaret has booked the cafe for your wedding reception. Thought that would bring a smile to your face! Now cheer up and don't think any different about what you are, for you are one of us. So make it snappy and get those cricket practice nets up. There are lots of clubs wishing to book their time in practice nets.'

Several weeks later, the building projects were almost complete and also garage workshops were complete, just a little cosmetic work was to be done on the cafe/restaurant and then it would be finished. Ray had overseen most projects and suggested to me that if I was away cricketing, he would watch over my department for it linked up with his fitness and health department.

I wished to be part of the team for England. Australians were coming over that summer, and I could be away playing cricket a lot.

'We will sort something out, Henry.'

'Ray, I want to know about the woman you were with last night.'

'Just a friend.'

'It looked a bit more than friends to me, Ray. Who is she then? Are you going to tell me?'

'If you must know, it's Hazel. Our solicitors daughter.'

'Those that represent us you know how to pick them, Ray. How did you meet her?'

'Mind your own business.'

'I know they come to you for a good massage or rub down.'

'Henry, o go before I give you a massage across your head.'

Joe called to say two police cars were coming in for repairs. Unless otherwise stated, police transport to be given priority and two traffic lanes to be left clear at all times for police emergencies. Floodlights were erected, and for insurance purpose, alarms were to be fitted throughout the premises. Then inspections had to be carried out for health and safety reasons, and fire escape areas had to be known to all. Then Jenny explained, 'There is an open day planned with garlands, buntings, coffee/tea, cakes, sandwiches, and a few more attractions.'

'When are you getting married Jenny?'

'Henry, you have asked Ray that. Now what's your game? You are up to something, but as you ask, it may be before you. Why?'

'I'm just curious that's all.'

'Henry, you are too curious. What is it with you?'

'Well, I think it'll be good for business for all of us. We must protect and expand as time goes on. We have an excellent start.'

'Blink, we will not fail. We are as one, and in business you'll find me a no nonsense business women and as hard as nails. But outside of that, I'll be as sweet as an apple pie. So, Blink – I'm going to call you Blink be like that for your cricket. Be a saint in the pavilion and a devil in the field. Does that answer you?'

'Jenny thanks. You will do fine.'

'Yes, Blink, I will. Like the Mafia, the family comes first.'

It took two weeks; all was up and running and everything was running smoothly. Ray was talking about further expansions. 'Jenny, what do you think? We are open 24-7, how about taxi service run from the garage?'

'Sounds fine, but we don't have the cars.'

'No, Jenny, drivers use their own as being self-employed. We'll have to apply for a license to operate, but I don't see any problem.'

'Ray, save it for the next meeting, but I think you have something there. I'll have a word with Joe. He perhaps can help us out on what's required from local authorities.'

Joe was contacted but was far too busy to listen, for night before the bank on High Street was robbed. They got away with £ 170,000. The robbers all wore balaclavas and gloves. Four of them were caught on CCTV before they sped away in a white van. 'We have the plate numbers, but the van was stolen.'

'What time was that, Joe?'

'Around eleven o`clock last night.'

'Come, Joe, follow me. Look, here we have them on our CCTV. They filled up or rather bought petrol, four gallons, and one came to the night window to pay and here he is. Seen that face before, Joe?'

'Not half, Jenny. You are a darling.'

'Not me, Joe. It's the night shift, Emma and Steve. You ought to talk to them.'

'Jenny, I wish to take the film and addresses of your staff. Ray, you know were Emma lives and Steve?'

'Of course I do.'

'I'm going to ring my boss and then see you later.'

'On CCTV, do you know the person?'

'Yes. It is Pete Tallon, only been out a couple of months. We'll keep you informed, but our men will be down for fingerprints. Did he have gloves on when paying?'

'Don't think so, but I was not there. Why? Oh, I know what you mean. Well, most payers put their hands on that night window shelf.'

'Good. Don't let anyone near it.'

'No, Joe. We use the main entrance during the day.'

'Right. In the meantime, I'll put that swing sign in front of the window to block it off. Our men will wish to check it out. See you later. Now what was it you wanted a word about?'

'We are thinking about running a taxi service. What do you think?'

'You apply to the council for the necessary forms. No leave it to me. I'll check it out. You're not in any hurry, are you?'

'It's for next month's meeting.'

'Right I'll see what I can do. Good idea, a taxi service to operate from here. You should do well. Jenny, if it's the same people on CCTV who robbed the bank, my boss will be pleased with you. They maybe miles away in another car, but we will get them. It's very difficult these days, robbing a bank. Everything is very technical for security reasons. That's why we think it's an inside job or assisted with inside information.'

Fingerprint experts, whilst checking things out, got a call to say the gang whilst refusing to stop after being chased for several miles south of Newcastle collided with stationary vehicles. Two passengers were killed, and two were taken to hospital. The money was retrieved. The one named Pete Tallon was killed.

At the garage, fingerprints were taken and the officers left, saying, 'We have all we require. You can open the night window when you wish. Our work here is finished.'

A few days had passed, and another suspected robber died in the hospital, and Joe arrested a bank employee who had assisted the gang with the security systems and knowledge of layout of the alarms; Joe received worthy praise for his work.

Jennifer questioned Joe on why people attempted something like robbing a bank. He said, 'Some people will do anything for money. They don't think about the consequences. Prison doesn't worry them. Some feel better off in prison. Whilst they're out of prison, they enjoy themselves until the money dries up. Then they get caught and go back to prison. Do they care? Not one bit! That's the system, and we, the police, just do our job. It's a circle that goes round and round. Some criminals, when sent down by a judge, say under their breath, "thank you". I've been in courts and seen it and heard it.'

'Joe, my job is to control the company, and I'm going to be tough but fair. We have it up and running and it looks good. I've Dad to thank for that for he waited to die before telling us anything about what he wanted us to do. We must respect his wishes, and Henry wishes to know when we're getting married.'

'Well, what did you tell him?'

'I said I'll ask you, but then it's you who should be asking me. Well, I'm waiting!'

'All right then. Will you marry me, Jenny?'

'Well, I might have to think about it – of course, I will.'

'Come here! Give us a cuddle.'

CHAPTER 13

Last of the Rambles

I APPROACHED MARGRET for a ramble on Sunday next week. 'I'm away at the nets for cricket practice, and then the season will be upon us and I'll not have a lot of spare time. So yes, we can ramble and enjoy ourselves if the weather is kind. Where shall we go and how many miles?'

'Five or six miles, and we can have lunch outside. We can start at village corner, go up to the lime quarry, turn left of Green Hat pub on to chestnut woodland, then over the canal bridge to cross roads down Courting Lane to Highwayman Pub for lunch. How does that appeal to you?'

Fine.

'Do you think you can keep up?'

'Margaret, I'll show you just how fit I am and I have to be in my job. I've been thinking, Margaret, with cricket being played in forty overs and twenty overs county games and England calling me up, I just cannot do all those games. Too much cricket is being played for test players. I know it's on the agenda at top level to try and make things easier.'

'Henry, you just wait and see what your employers make of it. It has created much interest and brought back supporters for exciting cricket and put more money back into the game, so in some respects, it's a good thing. So let the powers that be sort it out. Whatever you do, I'll support you. Just go and do what is expected of you.'

It was Sunday and we were all mustered, ready for a ramble. It was a spring morning with fine rain spreading across all areas with very little sunshine; what sunshine there was created shadows, a kind of awakening from dreary winter months of grey skies and short light days; a kind of feeling of a new life seemed to appear. People became more sociable in their greetings; animals and birds all seemed to sense something different was happening. It was spring – like a new world is born. People wished to cast off those heavy, dark winter clothes and put on lighter garments. Men brushed themselves down, combed their hair, and smartened up, and the women – like all living things – wished to make themselves attractive with make-up and fashionable clothes. Wild life sensed great changes, with birds singing and animals doing their calling – a great sense of communication. The environment was alive with the sound of activity.

On our way, we came through the chestnut woodland with squirrels noticeably dashing about the foliage and up and down the trees. An odd fox cunningly and slyly avoided interference in its way of life. Then it happened: several rabbits and a few foxes and many squirrels and weasels, and a deer pushing itself forward through the bracken, disturbing small birds, like robins, bullfinches, linnets, and hedge sparrows to mention a few – all congregated as if waiting for something to happen. Crows and jackdaws croaked loudly, and in the treetops, wood pigeons wooed all these creatures to come in one place. Margaret pulled out her camera, but a crow speared itself down from the treetops, attacked Margaret, and knocked the camera to the ground. A teammate picked it up, and again they were attacked by more crows; Margaret retrieved the camera and put it into her bag. Then the crows flew back into the treetops.

A member of the group stepped forward to have a closer look, but the animals and birds quickly disappeared and the rambler rejoined the group. Then the animals and birds returned. Margaret called me away from the group and whispered, 'That's the place you were found some twenty years ago.'

'Margaret, I don't feel threatened. I'm going to them. You stand well clear and be still.'

I removed my rucksack and carried it forward amongst the circle of creatures. I placed my rucksack down and sat on It. Quickly, crows sat on my shoulders. A robin perched on my head, and others jostled for a place on my lap. The deer forced its head forward for a stroke and a cuddle, and the stouts and weasels stood upright like meerkats. Suddenly a ray of sunlight shot through the treetops directly on me, highlighting my presence, and all went still and quiet. Not a sound was heard; a frightening stillness came over everyone. There was not a murmur, not a sound – so strange when a short while ago the woodlands were alive with animal sounds and the singing of birds.

I thought for a moment, 'What shall I do?' I sat in silence for a little longer; then I thought I heard someone call 'Henry! Henry, Henry'. I feared to answer; again there was a call of 'Henry' in a soft calm cool voice, a voice I had not heard before. 'Henry, I'm calling you. Why don't you answer?' I turned to the party of ramblers, but they gave me little response.

I whispered very quietly to the animals, 'What is it?'

The voice came back to me. 'I'm the Green Man of the forests and your friend. I wish you well in your marriage and cricketing career.'

I whispered, 'Come forward and show yourself I do not fear you. Why do you not show yourself?'

There was a tremble in the bracken, a lifting of leaves that had lain idly on the woodland floor through the winter months, a small breeze that made its presence felt on me, and then the voice replied, 'You feel my presence but do not see me.'

'Why don't I see you?' I cried.

'You have my presence' came, the answer.

'I feel you! Now show yourself.' Again there was a rustle of leaves.

'Henry, you live in a society that kills and eats animals. You hunt them down and then kill them. It is kill, kill, kill! You kill your own kind. You fight for peace. Those who survive, you give them medals. You cut down trees and build upon the land that much life depends on. You poison our waters with waste chemicals. You condemn mistreatment of the human race yet inflict pain and suffering. The list is endless. You swank and brag as if you own everything. It's not your world. You're only tenants. Other life has just as much right to be here as the people. You can be so cruel with your man-made laws that trespass upon our laws of nature.

'You have developed a brain that is most advanced of anything else on earth, yet you can destroy things with a flick of your fingers. You count your losses in manpower. What about our dear friends that surround you? What about our pollinating friends, our vegetation, and the air you breathe in? You foul it all up. Man must be the cruellest creature God created. You go into town centres and see our friends, the pigeons, begging for food, and you let your children attempt to kick them off the pavement or sidewalks and then laugh. You cage birds and then expect them to sing for you, and you, Henry, do neither. We know what you do and eat. You play cricket, and some of our feathered friends follow you to South Africa and other foreign places and come back to see you play over here. Now there is loyalty and support if ever there was.

'You wait for autumn, then hunt animals and birds and shoot them dead. You celebrate festive seasons with eating far too much, you fill yourselves like gluttons with meat, turkey capons, chicken, duck, lamb, pork, beef, veal, and many others – the list is endless – and then burb and go to the doctors, wondering what is wrong with you.

'You build great churches and then pray to God for a better life for yourself and others, and then go to war and kill, kill, kill, and kill again. Anything in your way, you kill. That's your religion. Now look into the eyes of that deer that you are stroking. Could you kill that and then eat it?'

'You, whoever you are, ask me questions, but give me no opportunity to reply. I ask, why have you left it so long in contacting me?'

'Henry, you are a man now. We did our job twenty years ago. We protected you, then gave you back to your people. Your rambling days are over. You will not see this place again after today, and you will prosper in whatever you do.' There was a flutter of feathers, a shaking of branches, a croaking of crows, a cooing of pigeons, and a short roll of mist. Then all was gone.

'Henry, what are you doing?'

'Margaret, did you hear and see all that?'

'See what, Henry?'

'All those animals and birds and hear that man?'

Everybody laughed.

'Henry, what world are you in? There is no one there. Now put on your rucksack. We have to move on, lost enough time. Now come on. You seem to be in another world. Snap out of it. No one is here. We have neither heard nor seen anything.'

'Margaret, I spoke with the Green Man.'

All laughed mockingly. 'There's no such thing. It's a rumour. You must not take any notice. We saw nothing.'

'You saw me sitting on my rucksack?'

'Yes, we did. You took out your wetsuit, put it on, and then picked a few wild daffodils and bluebells that one should not do.'

'What about those crows that attacked you?'

'Henry, nothing has attacked us, no crows here. Come! We have to go.'

'Margaret did you bring your camera with you?'

'Yes. I have it in my bag. Why?'

'Nothing. Maybe we'll take some photos later.'

A little further down the road I mentioned, 'You can believe what you wish, but I know what I know. And it's raining now, but it was sunny a while ago.'

'No, Henry, there has not been any sunshine all morning.'

'Well, Margaret, look back. Where is that smoke coming from? That's the place where I have been. It's burning.'

'Henry, are you not well? There is no smoke or fire. Now come on. The quicker we get to that pub for lunch the better. How do you feel, Blink? Are you having me on?'

'Why do you call me Blink? You have not called me that for ages?'

'Someone told me to.'

'Who told you?'

Someone over there.
No one over there.
'Blink, I saw and spoke to someone over there.'
'No, you didn't.'
'I tell you, I did.'
'You have me at it now. So come on, let's move on.'

CHAPTER 14

Play Up, Play Up, and Play the Game

LATER INTO SUNDAY evening I got to thinking about what had happened on the ramble and sought Ray out. 'What is it, Blink?'

'I wonder if you could run me over to the gypsy camp for I'm still working on my car and would like to have word with Rosie Knowles.'

'Pleased to see you, Blink. Would you like your fortune told?'

'No, Rosie. I wish to ask you something. Did you start any fires this morning in the chestnut woodland?'

'No, not us, Blink. Why, what is it? Blink, there's been a fire just off the road. If you go that way, you'll see.'

'I know, Rosie. What I wish to know, who started it?'

'Blink, when we passed at lunchtime, there was nothing but burnt bracken and grasses. I know the council are going to widen the road and put a lay-by in to accommodate three cars.'

'Rosie, was it raining early this morning about eleven o'clock?'

'It sure was. It started about nine, only steady until eleven, then it poured down.'

'Well, tell me how could a fire be burning as you say when it's raining fast? I saw great smoke rising high into the sky.'

'Henry, you are confusing me, and if there was a fire, so what?'

'Rosie, there are funny things happening. I'm getting confused. There seems some other power telling me what to expect and what to do, but I fear nothing, only concerned.'

'Are you all right for time, Henry?'

'Yes, Rosie. We are fine.'

'Then come this way. I show you something. By the way, Henry, have you still got the lucky charm I gave you?'

'Rosie, I wear it all the time along with neckerchief clip that was Nick's.'

'Fine now come, come, hurry or you may miss it. Look there. Do you see any rain?'

'No only blue skies.'

'Now look at the chestnut woodland. What do you see?'

'Rainbow.'

'Ray, do you see it?'

'We all see it, but there's no rain about.'

'Look at the end of the rainbow, the left side. Now what do you see?'

'That is where I was found.'

'Correct. Ray, do you see it?'

'I do.'

'Then you are a witness, but no one will believe you. And now it's gone, never to return, and the beam of light will never return. Now you believe what you want.

'You condemn us for begging, yet your doormats are full of begging letters and dodgy phone calls every day of the week. We gypsies have been persecuted since the birth of Christianity. You build churches then pray in them, and first chance you get, you nick lead off the roofs, not us gypsies.

'You are adapted to civilisation and to your way of life. We gypsies wish only to be free from the constraints of society, yet many of our people live amongst you. For many years, our painted horse-drawn caravans you have admired and now our modern caravans. We offer you good luck rather than bad luck. We are not demons or evil. We are people who wish to live a life different from yours, or is it you who wish to live a life different from ours? Now I have spoken. Go your way in life and be prosperous and have a good life and ask them when did they offer us a good life? We complain and become a nuisance. You complain and the answer is "We'll look into it". Good day, my friends.'

'Blink, I've seen with you, but no one will believe us. They'll think we need sectioning, maybe best not to say anything for a while.'

'Let's leave it at that for now. Ray, you say nothing to Margaret.'

We did not say anything to anyone. 'Ray, at the weekend I'm at county nets and don't want any distraction and then hopefully it's MCC against the old enemy, the Australians. I need to get my car on road. Will you help me?'

'No, but I know who will. Let them mechanics in the workshops look at it.'

'Good idea, Ray. I will.'

'And, Blink, any chance of any free tickets to the matches?'

'Why, am I not worth paying to see? If you don't pay how do you expect the public to pay? I'll see what I can do.'

It was now the end of May, and county cricket matches had started. I got the call for inclusion in the twelve against the old enemy, the Aussies. Margret was overjoyed and was going to take time out to be there to see the game.

The marriage was arranged for the end of the cricket season. 'Henry, you are not getting away with it this winter. We marry, whether you go on tour or not.'

'Margaret, I know we will, so don't worry. We can work around it somehow. So far, I'm pleased with my form. I must stay concentrated on my game. Thank you for putting the jar of honey in my cricket bag. I like to take a couple of spoonfuls during the game.'

For first test I was chosen amongst the twelve. It was the morning of the match, and I opened my cricket bag to find the book of poems by Sir Henry Newbolt. I picked it up and the pages opened to read 'Vitai Lampada' meaning 'The torch of life' and the words 'play up, play up, and play the game'.

First game, I opened with another left-hand batsman. We were to face two of the fastest bowlers in test cricket and the highest wicket takers. The ground was a sell-out, the crowd anticipating a good day of cricket under beautiful blue skies. The field was set, the batsmen were ready, and a hush fell upon the crowd. I got a run off the first ball, then another run was scored, and rest of the over was murderous as the balls flew through to the wicketkeeper.

That was first over. For next over, I had one run off the first ball, then played three deliveries back to the bowler, then two runs taken off the next delivery; last ball of the over I played a good cover drive, the ball going for a four. The ball struck a pigeon, and then it rolled to the boundary for four runs.

The pigeon lay motionless; a fielder picked it up to remove it from field of play. A voice said, 'Henry, go to it.'

I walked to the fielder with my hands outstretched to take the bird.

'It's dead,' said the fielder. 'I'll remove it from the field of play.'

'No, give it to me.' I took the bird, put my hand on it, and caressed it. Then the bird flew away after circling my batting area.

I stood my ground against the hostile bowlers; eventually, I was caught in the slips for fifty-two runs. It was a very tense game; England where 365 all out, first innings. Aussies were 369 all out first innings. It was England's second innings, and I heard voices. 'Keep playing forward. Wait for the bad ball. Keep your bat straight.' And so I did. I scored 104 and was caught on the boundary. We were all out for 447. Aussies were leading by 4 runs on first innings, making it 444 for the Aussies to win. I was hearing voices within my head, 'play up, play up, and play the game'. It was a long, hard day, trying to bowl the Aussies out until end was in sight; they were all out 43 runs short – a victory for England but far from easy. We had four more games to play as in test matches the best of five wins the series, but the glory for first test match went to England.

No one thought to ask me about the bird except the fielder who had retrieved it. 'That bird was dead when I picked it up. Then it flew away. I haven't seen anything like it. What did you do?'

'I just said a few kind words, and it just flew away.'

'I'm not believing that.'

'You say it was dead. What else could I do?'

'I don't know. It's very strange. Not seen anything like it before. I know what I saw, and my team mates are laughing at me. They don't believe me. You know that bird was dead. Will you tell them?'

'Look, my friend, it flew away, so it must be alive.'

'You did something. What was it? That bird was dead.'

'If that bird was dead, how could it fly away?'

The story circulated around the world; people wished to believe the bird was only concussed and woke up and flew away. They soon altered their indifferent thoughts when during other test matches hundreds of birds descended on the playing fields, not to interrupt the games; they just settled on boundary edges. As soon as the game commenced, they flew high over the wickets and then disappeared. Many just thought it to be a coincidence and natural, as freshly cut grass gives temptation to birds to forage. But not me, I know different.

Summer was coming to an end, and cricket matches were coming to their conclusions for the season. The 'torch of life' was going out. The series was a win for England and we reclaimed the Ashes. I was happy with my performance with the bat with a 58 run average. I claimed 'Man of the Match' in the third game and was declared the 'best young cricketer of the season'. There were many murmurs in the Aussie camp about me. I was the one to watch in future matches. I approached Margaret with the words: 'The curtain has fallen, the games are over, and I played up and played the games. The torch of life will dimmer, waiting for next summer. Margaret, let us get married.'

Arrangements made for our marriage, and the date was set for a simple marriage – nothing over the top, just things being straight and simple. The reception was to be at Jennies Place, then honeymoon in Paris. Several weeks passed; then the day arrived – a lovely sunny day. Many friends packed into the church to give witness to our marriage. Ray was best man, and I was heard to say 'Wish grandad was here'. I looked around and thought I saw him. Then my eyes fell on Rose Knowles, who just smiled and nodded in an agreeable way.

I got a feeling of great comfort and heard a voice say 'Henry, may you have much happiness'.

I turned to Ray and said, 'Thank you. That's very kind of you.'

'What? I didn't say anything.'

I suddenly recalled it was the voice of Grandad, but Grandad was dead. I was hearing voices again; then I was brought back to reality by the words: 'Do you, Henry Charles Bloom Black, take this woman to be your lawful wedded wife?'

'I do.'

Then it was 'You are husband and wife'.

At the reception, there were toasts of good luck and happiness with many handshakes until the car arrived to take us to the airport to go away to Paris. As we attempted to enter the car, doves settled on our shoulders and then turned their heads into my ears as well as Margaret's ears, as if passing a message. Then they flew into a circle around us both and disappeared. We left to honeymoon in Paris, leaving the congregation waving frantically behind the car; amongst them I noticed Rose Knowles smiling in approval with a face of agreement and satisfaction.

The End

www.ingramcontent.com/pod-product-compliance
Lightning Source LLC
Chambersburg PA
CBHW020401290526
45785CB00005B/2387

* 9 781479 749843 *